VINTAGE FAIRGROUND TRANSPORT

A personal collection

STEAM TRANSPORT

The Rodeo Switchback ride was moved from Fovant, near Salisbury to the Hollycombe Steam Collection near Liphook when ownership was transferred to the Fairground Heritage Trust. The move was carried out in traditional style with the ride being towed by Burrells 'Princess Mary' and 'Princess Marina', in September 1993

top right - 'Princess Marina' pulling through Wilton in the late evening
opposite - Ready to start the second part of the journey after an
            overnight stop at Salisbury cattle market
bottom right - Pulling up the hill out of Salisbury
below - 'Princess Mary' taking on water from the river at Stockbridge

John Wharton's Burrell King George VI undertook a mammoth task when it was used to tow the newly restored Carters Jungle Thriller Ark from ground to ground through the 2006 travelling season. The Ark was new to William Thurston Jnr. and opened by him in 1934. It was sold to Teddy Andrews in 1938. He travelled and worked the ride with Burrell 3489, which he named 'King George VI', from 1938 to 1948. This engine was later sold to S.J.Wharton of Minster Lovell, Oxfordshire.

The engine is now owned by John Wharton. By arrangement between the owner and Joby Carter, this Burrell was worked with the Ark during the 2006 season, re-creating the situation with Teddy Andrews nearly 70 years previously. The engine had to generate electricity to both light and power operation of the Ark when the Carters Steam Fair was open.

Here the engine is working at Hemel Hempstead over the Friday evening and the weekend of 14-16 July 2006.

EDWARDS OF SWINDON

Edwards of Swindon were a very well-known show family from before the mid-19th century. They retired from travelling and closed down their business in 1992. Several of the rides and transport items were sold to the Fairground Heritage Trust (FHT) and to the late Roger Austin, who was a major collector of ex-Edwards equipment. Roger also helped the FHT with storage of equipment and transport when the FHT went through difficult times in the late 1990s and early 2000s.

top opposite - Building up the Edwards Dodgem track from its packing trucks at the storage yard at Three Mills, East London in May 1994
bottom opposite - line-up of ex-Edwards Highwayman Scammells exhibited by the late Roger Austin at Stratford-upon-Avon 800th anniversary fair in 1996.

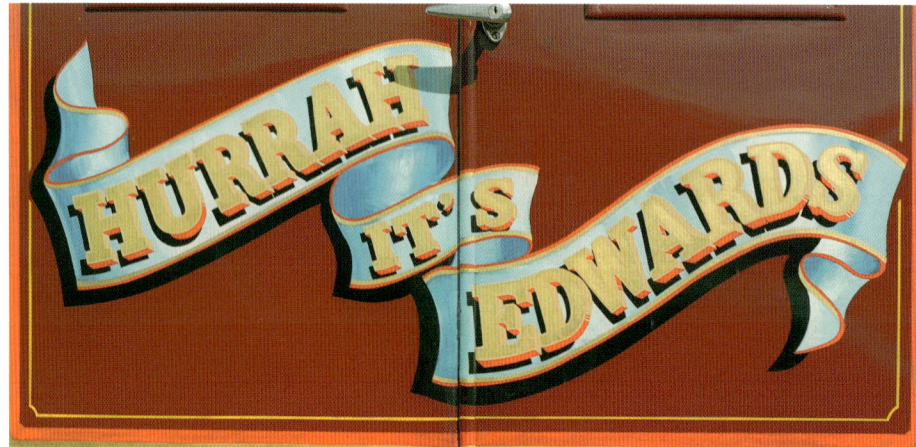

above - Edwards Dodgem packing trucks at the Fairground Heritage Trust new museum building at Dingles Steam Collection in May 2006. The nearest box truck, number 12, and the furthest, number 11, both date from 1947

right - Edwards Highwayman Scammell 'Moonraker' at Dingles, May 2006

opposite - Edwards Highwayman Scammell, also named 'Moonraker', fitted with a Showtrac type body conversion. This was seen at the Fairground Association of Great Britain's AGM at the late Roger Austin's premises at Raunds in April 1997

Flanagan's Showtrac Scammell at the Fairground Association of Great Britain AGM at the late Roger Austin's premises at Raunds in April 1997

Hibble & Mellor's Showtrac Scammell at the 'Showtrac Special' at Carters Steam Fair at Croxley Green in September 2005

Anderton & Rowland's Showtrac Scammell at Parham Steam Rally, near Storrington in June 1996

Russell Cook's restored ex-Pat Collins Showtrac Scammell at the 'Showtrac Special' at Carters Steam Fair at Croxley Green in September 2005

Only 18 Showtrac Scammells were made by the company. This special model for showmen was first produced in 1945. It had the generator fitted within the body and carried a winch.

A number of showmen had conversions made to a similar design, but the originals are rare and valuable units.

Anderton & Rowland's Showtrac Scammell's at the Fairground Heritage Trust fairground weekend at Dingles Steam Museum in September 2005

ex-Harry Wigfield's, originally Harniess' Showtrac Scammell at the late Roger Austin's, April 1997. Harry Wigfield purchased it from Frank Harniess in 1969.

Russell Cook's Showtrac Scammell at the 'Showtrac Special' at Carters Steam Fair at Croxley Green in September 2005

Bensons Showtrac Scammell alongside James Horton's gallopers at Parham Steam Rally in June 1996

Yorkshire showman George Tuby has a very well presented collection of three Scammells. There are two Highwaymen tractors converted to the Showtrac style. Here is one of these, in a line-up of all three, seen on display at Whitby carnival in August 2005

CARTERS STEAM FAIR

Carters Steam Fair present a superb set of prime movers, lorries and packing trucks used in transporting their fairground equipment and in generating power for rides, side stuff and living vans. The main fleet consists of Scammells, but there are also Atkinsons, ERFs, an AEC and this unique AA Ford. It is fitting that the Carter family and their regular tenants are given comprehensive coverage here for their unique set of transport, which is in everyday use throughout the travelling season.

1932 Model AA Ford, believed to be the oldest commercial vehicle working on a fair in Britain, used as a support vehicle for Candy Floss sales and as a display on the fairground. This view is at Hemel Hempstead in July 2006

Carters Scammell line-up at West Wycombe in May 2006

Another view of the line-up at West Wycombe in May 2006. Three ERFs are on the left.

Carters Scammell No.1 'Kathleen' in the yard after snow, January 2003

Carters Scammell No.2 'Mr Plod' ready to pull on at Winnersh, May 2000

Carters Scammell No.4 'Why Me' at Winnersh, May 2000

Carters Scammell No.3 'Old Ugly' ready to pull on at Winnersh, May 2000

Many of the Carters Steam Fair vehicles are shown on these and following pages. Fuller details of the history of each vehicle can be found on Carters website www.carterssteamfair.co.uk.

On these pages we show Scammells Nos. 1-4 and one of the Atkinsons. No.1 was built in 1951 for United Dairies, No.2 was built in 1957 and used by Esso, No.3 was built in 1967 for Stamp Transport. No.4 was built during World War 2. Atkinson No.10 was built in 1972 for Pickfords.

Carter Scammell No.6 'Why Worry' reversing living van into position at Pinkneys Green, May 2003

Carters Atkinson No.10 'The Queen' pulling Zed Carter's Vosper living van onto the ground at Pinkneys Green, May 2003

Carter Scammell No.15 'Perseverance' in the road (see moving blue van behind) waiting to pull on to the ground at Winnersh, May 2000. It was built in 1954 and carries a 5LW Gardner generator and Lister 110 volt dynamo

Carter Atkinson No.8 'The King', pulling on to Prospect Park, Reading in April 2000. It was built in 1973 as a road gritter. Its name relates to Anna Carter's painting of Elvis Presley on the signboard over the cab

Carter Scammell line-up at Marble Hill House, Twickenham, May 2003. From left to right - No.1 'Kathleen', No.14 'The Maidonian',
built 1960; No.6 'Why Worry', built 1961, No.12 'Victorious', built 1963, No.15 'Perseverence' and No.5 'Why Not'.

Carter AEC Mammoth Major No.11, built 1960, which was purchased with the ex-Tom Smith Octopus from Gerry Cottle, seen here at Chorleywood in 1994

Carter Scammell No.12 'Victorious', built in 1963 as an Arctic tractor unit

Peter Fleet's Scammell, carrying No.16, built 1951, at Hemel Hempstead in 2006. Peter Fleet has the Coconut stall on Carters fair

Carters Scammell No.14 'The Maidonian' at Winnersh in May 2000

Scammell No.14, fitted with a winch and crane, helps in building up the
Steam Yachts at Prospect Park, Reading, Easter 2003

Carter ERF No.13 and John Todd's ERF No.17 on display by the Dive Bomber at Marble Hill, Twickenham in May 2003. John is manager of the Dive Bomber ride and his wife Shelley runs the shooting galleries.

John Todd's Atkinson, No.18, by the Dive Bomber at Hemel Hempstead

TOM SMITH AUCTION SALE

As a complete contrast, these photos show some of the showmen's transport in the Tom Smith auction sale at Leighton Buzzard in November 1992. They illustrate how things can deteriorate when not used for many years. Most of these lorries were sold for spare parts, although a few were later reported as being restored by preservationists for rallying etc.

Two AEC's, signwritten as transport for T.Smith and Sons Super Dodgems

One of the several Scammells in the sale

Several of the lorries in the sale had been pulled from undergrowth at the rear of the yard

Scammell at the auction, complete with tree growing through the cab

MASONS

Masons is the trading name of the traditional fair operated by the Meech family. They are based in Reading and travel round the nearby Home Counties. Signwriting, scrollwork and other fairground art painting is carried out by Lee Meech.

One of Masons ERFs, signed as dodgem transport, seen at Wokingham in 2001

Masons ERF packing truck for the gallopers at Arborfield in July 2001

Jimmy Meech's Scammell 'Old Ted' at Goring regatta, July 1997. The gallopers seen are before their redecoration by Lee Meech, shown on the next page

Masons Foden with Lee Meech's gallopers in a summer thunderstorm,
Shinfield, July 2006

Line-up of Masons ERFs and the galloper packing truck, Wokingham, July 2006

Wareham's Atkinsons and Foden, together with the Anderton & Rowland Scammell
that they travelled, seen at St. Agnes Steam rally in Cornwall in 1993

WAREHAMS

The Wareham family travelled a number of traditional rides
in the West Country during the early 1990s. One of their
main attractions was the Jungle Speedway Ark that had
previously been at Pickmere Lake in Cheshire. They also
operated a set of swingboats.

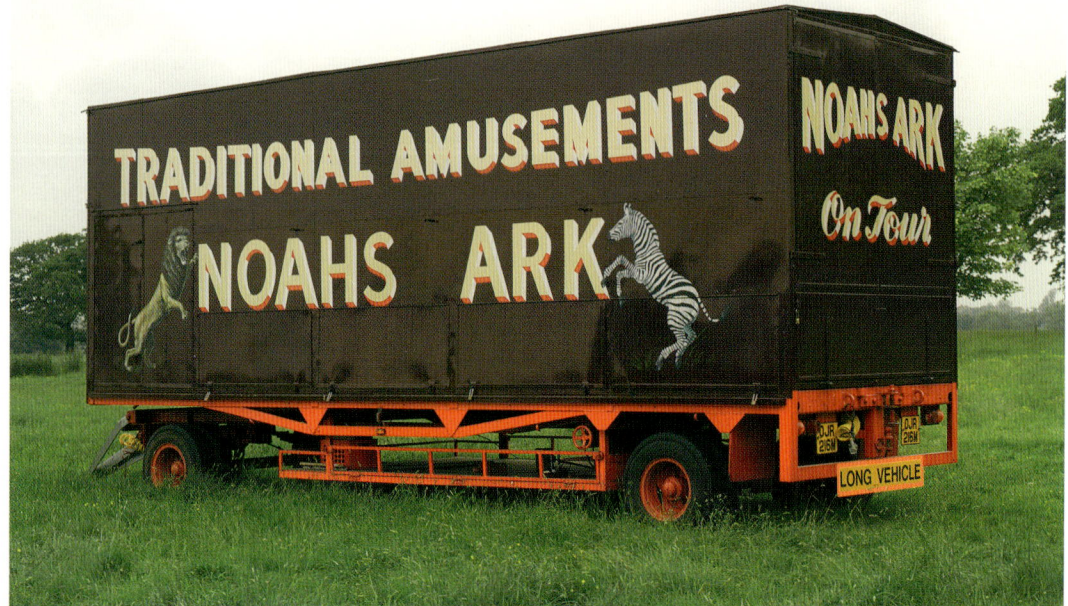

Wareham's packing truck for their Jungle Speedway Ark

Anderton & Rowlands Scammell 'Demetrius' operated by Wareham's, at Lydiard Park, Swindon in 1992

Russell Cook's ERF with Skid cars awaiting pull on at Prospect Park, Reading at Easter 2004

RUSSELL COOK

Russell Cook from Bridgnorth has a number of traditional fairground rides, including the ex-Frankie Harris Lakin Skid, ex-Beardow Gallopers, showmen's engines and other transport. His Scammell Showtracs appear on earlier pages. He has been an invited tenant with his Skid at Carters Steam Fair on several occasions.

Signwriting on Russell Cook lorry at Pinkneys Green in May 2003

Russell Cook's lorry carrying Skid components, seen at Prospect Park, Reading at Easter 2004

MIKE RULE

Mike Rule has an ERF and a Foden for transporting his steam gallopers to steam rallies and street fairs. Recently he has also acquired a traditional Helter Skelter (Slip), and repainted this in the style of the original amusements of this type. His handsome ERF transport for the Slip is seen below. Both photos were at Kemble Steam rally in August 2006.

HARRIS'S
ROAD TRAIN

MWV 153P

EXPLORER

SCAMMELL

Harris's Scammell is powered by a Rolls Royce engine instead of the more usual Gardner
engine. Seen here at Newick Green in 1992

Harris' pair of AEC Matadors at the village of Newick Green in 1992

The Harris Brothers from Ashington in Sussex travel their traditional rides - Gallopers, Dodgems, Ark, Chairs and Swingboats - mainly around Sussex and Kent. Their main transport comprises AEC Matadors and a Scammell.

Harris' FWD transport at the Bluebell rally in Horsted Keynes, Sussex in 1994

JOHN ARMITAGE

right - Cab and signage on John Armitage's Foden standing alongside his gallopers at Boston in May 1997

DORMANS

below - Dormans transport line-up for their Dodgems and newly restored Yachts, seen at Kemble rally in August 2006

HARRY CROOKES

right - The Matador on the right was Harry Crookes and towed his c1950 Rotor. It is seen here with the ride in 1992.

HARRY LEE

below - Harry Lee's 1948 AEC Matador was the prime mover for his Steam Yachts. The Matador photo was taken at the Coupland auction in October 2002. It was included in the lot for the Steam Yachts.

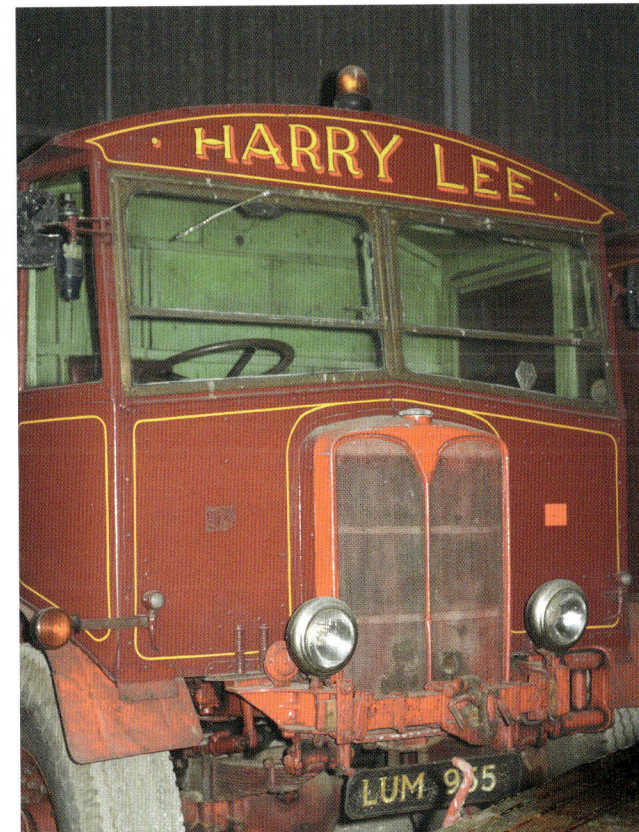

Matador vehicles were built by AEC during World War II for various military purposes such as towing guns, as generator trucks and as petrol tankers. After the war many were used for timber haulage and were also readily adopted by showmen. Over 9000 were built during the war and further batches were made post-war up until 1959.

JOHN BEACH

John Beach's Foden, used with his 'Disca Waltzer'. This was at Brocas Fair, Eton in 1993. Note Windsor Castle in the background.

HARRY WIGFIELD

Harry Wigfield travelled his earlier ex-Harry Gray Ark and his ex-Crows Royal Coronation Speedway Ark with his Showtrac Scammell for many years (seen earlier in this book when in the late Roger Austin's ownership). After the Scammell was sold in 1989 the Ark was travelled with this Atkinson, seen here at Irthlingborough in 1992.

Jack Schofield's Crusader Scammell and generators for his ex-Ashley Steam Gallopers. It is seen here at Blists Hill museum, Ironbridge in 1996. Jack also has another Crusader, which transports and generates for his Chair-o-Planes.

The intent in this book has been to show vintage transport in actual use by showmen rather than in preservation. Departing from this guideline, the final image is a salute to the many who restore and display these machines on the rally field. This is Colin Smith's restored Scammell at Pickering Steam Rally in August 2005